BIRMINGHAM'S JEWELLERY QUARTER

DEDICATION

With gratitude to the late Jill Mills and to
Sheila Dale who both encouraged me to make
my research public right from the start.

BIRMINGHAM'S JEWELLERY

QUARTER

Alison Gledhill

K.A.F. BREWIN BOOKS

First published in February 1988 by
K.A.F. Brewin Books, Studley, Warwickshire.

ISBN 0 947731 26 1

Cover Design: Mike Hill Graphics (0789) 69516.

Typeset in Baskerville 11pt.
and made and printed in Great Britain
by Supaprint (Redditch)Ltd.
Redditch, Worcs.

CONTENTS

LIST OF ILLUSTRATIONS

FOREWORD

In my years as editor of the trade journal *British Jeweller* I came across a number of histories of the Jewellery Quarter in Birmingham. When Alison asked me to look at yet another manuscript my agreement and goodwill was tinged with a certain amount of foreboding. Any fears were groundless; Alison has the mind of a researcher, plus the ability to marshal facts into straight-forward English. Her family connections with days past in the Jewellery Quarter have also helped in a project of feeling. As she prepares to take her place at Cambridge University my wish is that this book and her studies are but first steps in a long career with pen in hand.

Harry Bishop

January 19/1988

INTRODUCTION

This account of the Birmingham Jewellery Quarter, my first publication, has been fascinating to research and write, and by the nature of the work it has also proved to be a truly rewarding experience.

In its original form it was a school project on local history, and my choice of the Jewellery Quarter stemmed from family connections with the trade which I traced to my great-grandfather. For many of the anecdotal pieces which occur in the book I am grateful to my great-uncle, Ted Hopkins, who was born and bred in close proximity to the Jewellery Quarter, and to my grandmother, Elizabeth Hopkins. At this stage I would also like to thank Mr. Harry Bishop whose expert help and guidance has proved invaluable to me through all stages of this publication. I am also grateful to all the people in the Jewellery Quarter who supplied me with further background information and assisted me in my research.

Here follows a revised version of that original project which I hope proves informative, a pleasure to read, and perhaps even an incentive to delve further into the history of this industry, a legacy in the history of Birmingham itself. I am certain that there are stones which I have left unturned and facts which I have overlooked, and I apologise for this in advance, nevertheless, I hope to have highlighted some of the key aspects of the trade and its unique system and pattern of working.

December 1987.

The Growth of the Jewellery Industry in Birmingham 1773 to the Present Day.

As an industry in its own right, very little is known about the Birmingham jewellery trade in the years prior to 1773. This is because the Assay Office in Birmingham did not exist before then and all goods made were sent either to London, or to Chester to be assayed. This process of evaluation and hallmarking carried out elsewhere meant that no recognition could be given to Birmingham wares since they carried some other hallmark.

The trade began to expand at around the time of the arrival of the Birmingham Assay Office, although it was still secondary to the 'toy'-manufacturing and buckle-making industries in the area. This growth was due to Matthew Boulton's goods which enhanced the reputation of 'Brummagem wares' previously considered inferior in quality.

At the start of the nineteenth century when buckles became unfashionable, the Jewellery trade did not suffer; on the contrary it expanded. Larger firms encompassed many new branches of jewellery making, for instance the introduction of silver guard chain production in 1806. This was an important development because it marked the start of specialisation within the trade, upon which the whole character of the Birmingham industry has been formed. Craftsmen could break away from their parent firms when trade was good and set up individual works. The number of these separate enterprises increased because equipment was inexpensive, rents were low, and the great skill of these craftsmen sufficed for them to become masters in their own field.

The post-Napoleonic war depression of 1815 onwards hit the trade very hard. In 1825 it was close to extinction but was saved by Queen Victoria's accession to the throne in 1837, when the wearing of jewellery became fashionable once again.

1840 marked a revolution in the Jewellery Quarter with the discovery of an effective method of electro-

Matthew Boulton's Soho Manufactory, built in 1864. Boulton and his building were the key to raising the standard of Birmingham wares.

plating which was the culmination of fifty years of experiments in this field. John Wright, in conjunction with George Richards Elkington, co-partner with his cousin Henry of Elkington's works, discovered the new method of electro-plating which was probably battery-based, but which also used a different conductive fluid, or electrolyte.

It was patented by Elkington's works and it soon superseded the more antiquated battery method of silver-plating because it was less erratic and less expensive. The old method soon died out as the Elkingtons monopolised the plating market and this section of the trade expanded in response to a demand from the 'status-seeking' Victorian middle classes who wanted imitation jewellery, virtually indistinguishable from real godl or silver. Hence the rolling mill, stamp and press, die-sinking, embossing by machine and decorative processes all evolved in Birmingham in connection with the mass production of plated, cheaper jewellery.

Specialisation had begun at the turn of the century. The face of the trade underwent a second change which was visible by 1865. The core trades of gold and silver-smithing, electro-plating and jewellery manufacture experienced a sub-division into smaller branches whereby separate, smaller firms supplied specialist services to the core trades; for instance they supplied gold chains, or studs and links, and after 1866, die-sinking, which was the moulding of metals stamped by machine into the shape of the die, became a specialised area of production.

The trade was flourishing, with the number of working craftsmen standing at 7,500. Employees earned a fair wage and settled down, generally speaking, into the mould of being "staid, quiet, respectable people", the sort of people who made the Jewellery Quarter the incarnation of these words, spoken by Sir William Ashley:

"The industrial greatness of Birmingham is the creation of a virile and enterprising individualism".

The nature of the work in the Jewellery industry is one which subjects it to extreme fluctuations in prosperity. The period after 1866 until the grave depression of 1886 became known as the 'Silver Jewellery Period' when the gold jewellery section lost some ground to silver during this time. Precious stones were increasingly used while imitation jewellery production remained static. New branches including the manufacture of official insignia like ceremonial keys, mayoral chains and the making of watch cases by machinery were also introduced. This

Silversmith's advertisement of circa 1840 when the revolution in
electro-plating took place.

increased the working capacity of the trade to 16,000.

The genius behind the making of watch cases by machinery came from an American, Aaron L. Dennison. He was the founder of the famous Dennison Watch Case Co. Ltd., in 1872. Improvements in stamping machinery and press tools for electro-plating were moving forward and the newly-invented gas engine was beneficial to the trade in general. By 1886 most workshops were served by this economical and commodious source of power.

Depression in 1886 came about through jewellery becoming unfashionable, and through speculation and reckless trading leading to bankruptcy. The trade gradually surfaced from this depression but revival was short-lived when the Prince Consort died in 1892 and jewellery became unpopular once again.

Strikes and slack trade in 1893-4 kept the industry in a rut but thereafter it had a new lease of life.

In 1887 the Birmingham Jewellers' and Silversmiths' Association was formed to protect and promote the trade. In 1888 it set up the Jewellers' School to educate trainees within the industry. The Association celebrates its centenary this year, in 1987, within the British Jewellery and Giftware Federation.

At the turn of the twentieth century gold jewellery, especially ladies brooches, was more popular than silver jewellery, and silver prices fell as world production increased. Silver was so readily available that it was used to make small articles like brush backs and it also began competition with electro-plating in the tableware branch of the trade.

New branches set up at this time included the production of ornamental medals, cups and shields with a view to catering for the new trend towards sporting competitions. Precious stones, especially diamonds were also favoured, mainly because this stone fluctuated very little in price when compared to the inconstancies in the price of other precious stones. Consequently diamond-mounting and gem-setting in general had become major branches of the trade.

The first decade of this century saw a rise in silver prices, a dip for the trade in general in 1908, a rally, and then trouble with the death of King Edward VII in 1910. This was soon rectified when the Coronation boosted orders for jewellery, commemorative medals and other memorabilia. Prosperity prevailed right up until the outbreak of war in 1914, peaking in 1913 when the number of employees was such that the trade ranked second in importance in Birmingham, next to the group of non-ferrous metal trades.

From 1903 up until the outbreak of war, The Jewellers' Association led by Mr. Joseph Chamberlain, organised a campaign to create an honest reputation for Birmingham jewellery in the light of the inferior quality of foreign competition which was penetrating the British market and bringing standards down. The results were positive and the campaign continued after the war.

The Association also began a Vigilance Committee sparked off by a rise in local crime in 1888. The aim of this Committee was to try to prevent the heavy losses felt by the industry as a result of theft and burglary of wares, or the taking of gold filings by employees. The committee and its 'vigilants' offered safety advice to employers to reduce their losses, but no concrete steps could be taken until the police had the legislative powers to be able to identify an offender. This finally material-ised in 1914 with a clause in the Birmingham Corporation Act which brought many offenders to trial.

Prevention of theft of gold filings was a more delicate matter; as little temptation as possible was, and is, proffered to the workmen who have always been of a superior class, and indeed theft (from within) has always been minimal compared to burglary (from without). Nevertheless there is a delightful story recorded at the turn of the century about a gold worker who was noted for continually rubbing his fingers through his greasy hair. When watched it was discovered that his nightly hair wash would involve allowing the dirty water to run through a flannel, thus catching all the gold dust!

The precautions against theft usually sufficed, how-ever. Workers wore large leather aprons fastened to the table to catch any filings and they were obliged to wash their hands in a special tank and have the gold article weighed before and after filing.

My great-uncle, Ted Hopkins, mentioned an inter-esting fact about wooden floors in gold workshops when they changed hands. Apparently, the floors were "bartered for" separately because of the gold dust that would be on the floor; the new owners would "fetch it all up and burn it and the bits they got out would cover the cost of that and a new floor!"

He also described the Quarter at its all-time peak just before the First World War: "At dinner times and mornings and especially on Saturdays, to try and walk on the footpath in the Jewellery District was absolutely impossible. It was just like thousands of people coming down across the road here. You've never seen anything like it. It was as good as any football match; it was massive."

With the advent of the war, abnormal circumstances and working conditions were the order of the day, demonstrating the mobility of labour in the Quarter. Many employees were called up, gold was restricted and some jewellers made munitions instead of jewellery; the number of employees in the district was thus cut drastically. The Jewellery Munition Committee supervised munition work, and working hours were divided between the manufacture of munitions and jewellery. Enough jewellery was made to capitalise on an opening in the South American jewellery market, almost totally monopolised by Germany before the war, and a shipment of Birmingham exhibition pieces set off for South America only to be torpedoed and sunk. In a second attempt at winning some of this market the Birmingham exhibition happily proved successful.

For those firms unable to obtain government work, however, the war meant financial ruin. In 1916, one newspaper described the war-stricken trade thus:

"You may go into workshop after workshop and see one side tenantless, idle, machinery still, tools lying on the bench. There is only one simile that leaps to mind. It is that of a body paralysed down one side."

On the other hand, the section of the trade with work in medals, badges and engraving experienced expansion and not bankruptcy.

A post-war boom ensued until 1920 with replenished labour from disabled ex-servicemen and sufficient availability of raw materials, but depression set in by 1921. Jewellery became unfashionable, the price of silver fluctuated, the export trade was depleted and more particularly the home trade contracted as general industrial depression set in and people became less extravagant.

During the General Strike of 1926 the association urged its members to work as normally as possible and a telegram of support was sent to the Prime Minister. Trade was so slack in 1927 that the Association drew up a jewellery advertisement slogan:

"GIFTS THAT LAST"

This heralded a Christmas rush which kept the trade on its feet.

The 'British Jeweller' magazine was set up in 1933 as

a means of advertising British wares and it is still going strong today, producing 7,000 copies each month.

1937 was the Golden Jubilee of the Birmingham Jewellers' and Silversmiths' Association celebrated by a commemorative booklet, a Ball and dinner and an exhibition at the Birmingham Art Gallery.

The Second World War brought hard times to the trade; some firms had to manufacture military equipment including badges and buttons and many workers were involved actively and passively in the War Effort. In 1940 supplies of all materials were limited sharply by the Board of Trade and special limitations were applied to gold wedding rings which were hard to come by. In 1941 the trade practically ceased to exist since munition production had taken over and smaller firms faced being engulfed by larger ones; indeed ten small firms were forced into "concentration", as it was called. The only wares made at this time were "utility articles" for the War Effort, but for some firms this meant liquidation and a special licence had to be introduced to allow them to stay in business.

By the end of the war the Sectional Reconstruction Committee set up by the association in 1943 had a great deal of work to do in reconstructing bombed-out premises. It also set forward proposals for redevelopment of the Quarter, beginning with the plan for a large flatted factory which eventually materialised into the Hockley Centre, opened in September 1971.

1946 saw the renaming of the B.J.S.A. to the B.J.A., standing for the British Joint Association of Goldsmiths', Silversmiths' Horological and Kindred Trades. This association built up its activities and strengths in line with regrowth of the Trade itself after the war.

Plan for the flatted factory which became the Hockley Centre.

Grant of Arms, 1950:
the British Jewellers' Association
Coat of Arms.

In 1950 a Letters Patent was granted allowing the use of Arms by the Association and a new badge and chain of office for the President was made to commemorate this; these items are used by the President of the current British Jewellery and Giftware Federation.

The 1953 Coronation hallmark was 'monopolised' by the Association and a ban on imported souvenirs imposed to protect the interests of the British industry.

During the 1950's controls on gold were alleviated by the Association and the 1960's saw a drive for a Federation which could fairly represent all sections of the trade. This resulted in the formation of the British Jewellery and Giftware Federation Ltd., commencing on 1st January, 1970.

The 1973 Hallmarking Bill introduced a platinum hallmark for the first time and old Acts of Hallmarking were completely amended to offer a more modern hallmarking system working to increase customer protection.

Silver Jubilee year in 1977 gave a boost to the industry and it also marked the commencement of funded research at Birmingham University to discover an alloy giving tarnish-free silver; perfection in this field has not yet been achieved.

The Government's Inner City Partnership Scheme was introduced in 1979 with grants for council redevelopment. Set against this positive step forward was the rise of gold and silver prices at the end of the year. The unprecedented problem arose of what to charge customers in the light of such an unstable situation. It was decided that jewellers should charge at the price on the date of order. Prices soon dropped as quickly as they had risen. The public lost confidence and a recession set in in the early 1980's.

The situation to date points towards rejuvenation of the industry. 1986 Assay Office statistics, without a break down on individual Assay Offices around the

9

country, show good home and export trading figures.

The number of traders in the Quarter runs in the region of several hundred and membership of the British Jewellers Association section of the Federation in its centenary year stands at nearly 800.

On top of all this, 1987 has been designated 'British Jewellery Year' and publicity drives aiming for increased public awareness have been continuing throughout the year, headed by the logo which was strikingly designed to promote this aim.

Logo used for British Jewellery Year, 1987.

Location of the Jewellery Quarter

The manufacture of jewellery in Birmingham evolved from an essentially domestic situation to that of a full-blown industry. The necessity of the various branches of the industry being within close proximity of one another is of paramount importance. Jewellery production is a closely-linked operation; for example, one ring may travel to several specialist shops before final completion.

Right up until 1746 the land around New Hall, the family seat of the Colmores, was divided up into freehold ownership. In 1746, Ann Colmore obtained an Act of Parliament permitting her to rearrange the New Hall estate and grant leases.

Many buckle-makers, jewellers and 'toy'-makers quickly took over the houses on the estate and the post 1770 years saw a densely industrial district shaping up to become the Jewellery Quarter proper a century or so later.

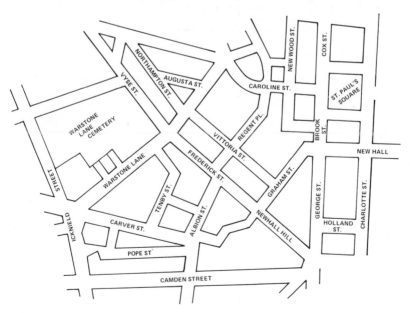

During the 1830's and 40's land prices soared and many jewellers had to move away from the canal, north of Great Charles Street to the Summer Lane, Constituion Hill area. The trade expanded, with increasing demand for cheap trinkets during the 1840's and 50's and aspiring jewellers moved eastward to the residential area of Vyse Street, Warstone Lane, and St. Paul's Square, so avoiding unnecessary renting of premises. Eventually entire streets of houses in the Hockley area were converted into workshops to form the traditional centre of the industry.

The spatial proximity of the Quarter provided a perfect system for an industry which, with its many subdivisions and suppliers, was highly inter-dependent between one section and another. Indeed a survey carried out in 1948 revealed the core of the trade as vaunting the highest density of industrial land usage in Britain. Only a few of the larger more self-sufficient firms have moved to the suburbs, still leaving the traditional centre intact.

'The War Stone'

War Stone in Warstone Lane which gives the road its name used to mark the town boundary. The writing inscribed on the base of the rock explains its presence and reads thus:

'The War Stone'

This felsite boulder was deposited near here by a glacier during the Ice Age, being at one time used as a parish boundary marker, was known as the Hoar Stone of which the modern War Stone is a corruption.

The Jewellery Quarter Clock the best know landmark in the district.
The clock stands at the junction of Warstone Lane and Vyse Street
and was erected by public subscriptions to commemorate the visit of
the Rt.Hon. Joseph Chamberlain, M.P. to South Africa in 1903, just
after the end of the Boer War. The Lord Mayor accepted the clock
on behalf of Birmingham City in January 1904. Mrs. Chamberlain
unveiled and started the commemorative clock on this occasion.

The Buildings in the Jewellery Quarter

The character of the Jewellery Quarter and its unique
history is reflected in the varied styles of architecture to
be seen up and down its largely residential, Victorian-
looking streets.

The unusual beginnings of workshops run within
domestic dwellings has already been mentioned, and
besides the cheaper rents involved, the accommodation
and lighting for jewellery production on a small-scale was

13

An excellent example of a type 2 building: number 46 Frederick Street.

A good example of a row of type 1 buildings as seen in Albion Street, which have undergone renovation.

The Argent Works, a type 3 building found on the corner of Legge Lane and Frederick Street.

not much different from what was needed for everyday life.

The buildings in the Quarter can be roughly sorted into three groups, with some buildings worthy of special mention. There are those converted from houses by enlarging windows and infilling the garden or yard at the back with 'shopping'. 'Shopping' is extra brick workshop buildings ranging from 1—3 stories high.

Secondly, there are the purpose-built workshops which lead on to the street with 'shopping' at the back and the front section often serving as offices or showrooms. These buildings are not dissimilar from suburban-type houses in appearance.

Finally there are the less commonplace large factories or workshops, of no specific design, which stand out because of their size and singularity.

Type 1 building
Albion Street, recently renovated.

Type 2:
No. 46, Frederick Street.

Tyep 3:
Argent Works (corner of Legge Lane and Frederick Street)

The Argent works brings architectural brilliance to the Jewellery Quarter with its Renaissance Florentine style of multi-coloured brickwork, Italianate towers and symmetrical lines. Besides this, the building also has an interesting history.

It was designed by J.G. Bland and constructed in 1863 for W.E. Wiley, a gold pen and pencil manufacturer. Each floor was built of hollow bricks with wrought-iron tiles passed through them. Bland stated that this doubled the weight-bearing capacity of the floor and made the building fireproof too; insurance was thus inexpensive.

The factory housed over 250 workers, some of whom worked in the section of the building given over to a Turkish bath which used Wiley's recycled steam from factory boilers. This is how a contemporary described the bath:

> "The rooms have been fitted up at very considerable
> cost; the floors are covered with Indian matting;
> luxurious couches are ranged along the walls;
> billiards, chess, fencing and other amusements are
> provided; and nothing has been omitted that could
> add to the enjoyment of the bathers!"

This amenity has now gone and the restored building now houses separate units for small businesses of various descriptions, including hairdressing. The units are rented on a monthly, all-costs-inclusive basis. As the Quarter adapts to change and looks to the future, the Argent Centre is a perfect example of how the old and the new can work economically together.

The Hockley Centre

The Hockley Centre was opened in September, 1971 as a flatted factory in an attempt to redevelop and modernise the Quarter. 150 businesses were displaced by the Centre and the intention was for them to be rehoused there. Only a few managed this, however, because rents were higher and the building attracted other commercial trades from the city centre. Many firms folded and others then searched elsewhere for a site.

The lesson learned in this event was that displacement meant ruination for many firms and this was too high a price to pay for modernisation's sake. As a consequence the Quarter became an 'Industrial Improvement Area' in April, 1980 and grants for improvement are available for proprietors from the authorities.

Other places of interest within the Quarter which highlight how close-knit the industry is, include the existence of the Mint, the Birmingham Assay Office and the British Jewellers' Association building, all within the area of the 'Hockley Square Mile', as it is known.

The Victoria Works lying between Frederick Street and Victoria Street is the earliest surviving purpose-built manufactory which was built in the late 1830's as a pen factory for one J. Gillott, a pioneer in making steel pen nibs by machine. The Works is now sub-divided into separate workshops but still remains in its original form of central courtyard surrounded by three sides of 'shopping'.

Clearly, then, there lies a story behind the history of the vast majority of the buildings in the Jewellery Quarter, which makes it a fascinating place to walk through. To crown its uniqueness, the Quarter boasts St. Paul's Square which formed part of the original Newhall estate developed by the Colmores in the late 1770's, and which is the *only* 18th century square in the City. The large properties built around it were all similar in style, occupied originally by families of professionals and only a few jewellers.   Rents were high because exclusive properties unthreatened by the fast industrialising town were few and far between and much sought after by the newly-rich. The Square remained untouched until 1840 but the need to convert houses into workshops meant that by the mid-nineteenth century, St. Paul's had lost its domestic function.

Today St. Paul's stands refurbished having undergone a huge facelift under the Quarter's Improvement Scheme; the Churchyard, the buildings around the square have been improved, some have returned to their residential function, and new building work has been completed.   The Church itself needs to be cleaned up, but the majority of work which needed doing in The Square has been accomplished. The emphasis now is not on bulldozing down but building up.

St. Paul's Church, 'the Jewellers' Church'
in St. Paul's Square, Hockley.

The Birmingham Assay Office

Silversmithing in Birmingham did not begin on a large scale until the eighteenth century when the makers of small metal items began to produce additional silver articles, like watch cases and spurs. The establishment of the Assay Office in 1773 marked the starting point proper of a trade which was already thriving. Henceforth the trade expanded and gained a just reputation for wares of quality and excellence.

Matthew Boulton, described by Lord Shelburne as "the most enterprising man in different ways in Birmingham", inherited the family buckle and button-making business in 1759 and developed the family Snow Hill plot into the Soho factory, completed by 1762. The fine quality silver wares were sent to the Chester Assay Office, 72 miles away, to be hallmarked. Hallmarking, as a way of protecting the consumer from fraud and the trader from unfair competition, had existed as a statute from a early as 1300 during the reign of Edward I. Boulton found this situation unsatisfactory. He gained no acclaim for his fine work and there were delays and damage to his wares on the journey which inhibited trade. He therefore petitioned Parliament, backed by other Birmingham silversmiths and on Lord Dartmouth's advice as a Secretary of State, to authorise an assay office in Birmingham.

Sheffield smiths felt the same way as their Birmingham counterparts so that petitions from Sheffield and Birmingham stating their cases reasonably both arrived at Parliament in February, 1773. The London traders feared for their grip on business if two new assay offices were to be introduced so they counterpetitioned their new rivals with such "exsufflicate and blown surmises" as the suggestion firstly that "deceit" would creep into the trade and ruin reputations and revenue; secondly that there were few skilled smiths in the areas proposed for the new offices; and following this wild conjecture came their third objection, which was the true root of their fears, that the new offices would prove detrimental to the financial security of the London branch of the trade.

18

A review committee and a committee of enquiry into existing Assay Offices were set up to assess the situation. The result was that existing assay offices suffered severe reprimands for breach of duty, the Act was eventually passed and Royal Assent given in Boulton's favour. He returned to Birmingham with local churchbells announcing victory. Boulton was the first manufacturer, with his partner, John Fothergill, to enter their marks.

The Assay Office's humble origins were in leased rooms in the Kings Head Inn, New Street. It moved to Bull Lane in 1782, then to Little Colmore Street in 1799, Little Cannon Street in 1915 and finally to the purpose-built site in Newhall Street, occupied from 1877 onwards.

The Birmingham Assay Office, situated in Newhall Street.

The Assay Office as an institution established by law is there to prevent fraudulent sales of gold and silver using unofficial hallmarks. It also enforces the hallmarking laws, and decides if an article must be assayed or not, issuing its decisions to the Trade.

Old and complicated hallmarking laws were brought up-to-date with modern-day jewellery production in 1973 with the Hallmarking Act of that year. It introduced a platinum hallmark for the first time and offered increased protection for the consumer in various ways; it specified sponsors' marks, made dealers obliged to display information about hallmarks, determined the trade description of gold, silver and platinum, defined what additions, adjustments and repairs could be made without the need for the article to be re-assayed and it also set up the British Hallmarking Council which guaranteed assaying facilities and oversaw the enforcement of the new law.

The actual processes of assaying and hallmarking are co-ordinated procedures. An assayer is a highly skilled, scientifically trained person who tests the purity of any article said to be gold, silver or platinum since all three metals are almost always combined with baser metals to strengthen them; the assayer thus checks the ratio of precious metal with combination metal.

A sample is taken by scraping various parts of the article. If the article is gold, the sample is weighed, heated in a cupel — a small crucible of bone ash — to $1,100^{\circ}C$ with silver three times the weight of the gold, both metals being wrapped in lead. The heating process separates the alloy base metals from the gold and silver and then these two are "parted" by being boiled in nitric acid in a platinum cup. The silver dissolves and the pure gold is left; it is annealed, or heat treated and then cooled slowly, until it is malleable and soft, and then it is weighed. The comparison of the first weight with the second weight reveals the proportion of gold to the alloy metal. The standard of the gold, its quality, is thus reached and is called its carat. One carat is the equivalent of one part in 24, thus 22 carat gold has 22 parts gold to 2 parts alloy, 9 carat gold has 9 parts gold to 15 parts alloy, and so on.

Silver is assayed using the 'wet' method, as opposed to the 'dry' or 'cupellation' method used for gold. The silver is dissolved in nitric acid, chemicals are added and eventually a precipitate is obtained. The clear liquid is compared to a standard colour sample of silver in this form — if it is darker than the standard sample, the silver under scrutiny is substandard.

The quality of silver is measured with two standards. Sterling silver is 92.5% pure and Britannia silver is 95.84% pure. The latter standard was introduced to prevent the melting-down of silver coinage in order to make silver wares. By contrast, platinum has a single standard of .950 platinum to .050 alloy metals.

Originally gold and silver were assayed using the touchstone method. This involved rubbing the article with a touchstone and comparing the colour of the sample with that of standardised articles, but this method is now extremely old-fashioned and more than likely obsolete.

Any substandard articles are broken up and returned to their maker. Articles meeting the criteria set by the Assay Office are then hallmarked. A hallmark consists of

A table of Convention Hallmarks

Precious Metal		Common Control Mark	Fineness Mark
Gold	18 carat	750	750
	14 carat	585	585
	9 carat	375	375
Silver	Sterling	925	925
Platinum		950	950

Special marks apply at authorised Assay Offices in the U.K., Austria, Finland, Sweden and Switzerland which are recognised under an International Convention. The mark consists of a Sponsor's Mark, a Common Control Mark, a numerical Fineness Mark and an Assay Office Mark (no Date Letter).

Marks indicating a silver standard below 925 Sterling are not approved for items in the U.K. Other countries marks are often those struck by the manufacturer. These do not indicate British or Convention hallmarking approval.

British Articles

Standard	From 1975
22 carat gold Marked in England	916
18 carat gold Marked in England	750
14 carat gold	585
9 carat gold	375
Sterling silver Marked in England	
Marked in Scotland	
Britannia silver	
Platinum	

Imported Articles

22 carat gold	916
18 carat gold	750
14 carat gold	585
9 carat gold	375
Sterling silver	925
Britannia silver	958
Platinum	950

Silver Jubilee 1935

Coronation 1953

Silver Jubilee 1977

four marks which grade the quality of the article. Gold articles firstly carry the sponsor's, or maker's mark which is registered and approved by the Assay Office, then there is the standard mark designated for each carat, next comes the Assay Office mark where the article was assayed and finally there is the date letter. This changes each year and appears in different series or ꞌ ycles where the alphabet is reproduced following a speꞌ fic design.

Silver articles carry the maker's mark, the Assay Office mark, the lion passant if it is sterling silver, or the figure of Britannia if it is Britannia silver, and ultimately the date letter, as for gold articles. Other hallmarks exist for imported articles and for special editions like the Royal Jubilee, or a Coronation.

Platinum carries the same marks as gold and silver articles, except that its standard is symbolised not by a lion, or a crown (used for gold) but by an orb.

The Assay Office marks show at which of the four offices in England the article was marked, either London, Sheffield, Edinburgh or Birmingham. The Birmingham mark is the symbol of an anchor which was perhaps taken from the name of the inn where much discussion and dealing had been done during the passing of Boulton's bill.

The Inn was called the 'Crown and Anchor'. It is said that the Birmingham and Sheffield parties tossed up between the two symbols and that Birmingham won the Anchor, Sheffield gaining the Crown.

Hallmarking occurs prior to any final fittings or furnishings on the article but if the article is too fine, or

The Anchor Hallmark as seen on the wall of Birmingham's Assay Office.

too small or awkward to hallmark, it is either left or marked several times earlier on in its manufacture, perhaps before soldering together. The craftsman can decide the position and size of the mark, but final approval must be given by the Assaymaster. All articles made of combined platinum and 18 or 22 ct gold have to carry both standard marks.

Consequently the co-ordinated and sometimes complicated procedures of assaying and hallmarking may take a long time, but since 1980 an Express Service has been in operation for the benefit of manufacturers with top priority orders, especially around Christmas time. It has proved a success and marks the willingness of the Assay Office to move with the times. The good relationship between the Assay Office and the B.J.A. continues, as it has done since the very beginning, to work for the benefit of the trade by maintaining high standards and sustaining the excellent reputation of Birmingham goods.

The Birmingham Mint

The Birmingham Mint is the longest-running private mint still in operation today. Ralph Heaton I, owner of a brass foundry and button-making business in Slaney Street operated there from 1794 until 1808 when business expanded and he moved to Shadwell Street. All of his sons worked in the firm and Ralph II, the youngest son, was given land on the Bath Street corner where he worked independently of his father as a die-sinker.

Ralph I died in 1832 and Ralph II's business expanded. By 1850 all the skills needed for minting were available to the Heatons, so they bought Soho Mint equipment from Matthew Boulton at an auction and set it up at the Bath Street shop, with Foreign Office Approval.

Orders arrived and the combination of acquired skills and new equipment was put to good use making coins for the home market and for export to the Colonies. The first order came from Australia for mercantile tokens and the first foreign order was from Chile in 1851 when the now-familiar 'H' mark first appeared. This was the beginning of a company which has evolved as the mint we know today in Icknield Street. In the same year the Royal Mint put in its first orders, so starting an association which still exists today with Birmingham and the first commemorative medal was made for the Crystal Palace Exhibition.

In 1852 the Birmingham Mint helped equip the Marseilles Mint for recoinage in France. This was the first time bronze coins were ever stamped, and English coinage changed metals from copper to the new bronze in 1860. The Marseilles venture with the MA mintmark folded in 1857.

In 1853 the Heaton mint took on copper coinage for the Royal Mint and in 1855 striking presses changed from heavy screw to the new efficient lever presses. The Bath Street Mint remained busy and required a fifth new press. More space was needed for this so that in 1860 the factory site in Icknield Street was bought and building work completed by 1862. Ralph II died the same year,

The Birmingham Mint and Crest, Icknield Street.

a year in which the company was also awarded the International Exhibition Medal for "Excellence of Many Coins".

Ralph III assumed control at the age of 35 and reigned supreme while the mint's foreign output was still high. In 1864 the mint contracted its first export of equipment to Burma and this decade saw much trade with Italy, Hong Kong and Romania. The Birmingham Mint soon superseded the Royal Mint with modern machinery and a higher coinage capacity and this supremacy took the company into the 1870's when the demand for colonial coinage was acute.

The Royal Mint, plagued with machinery problems subcontracted the Heaton mint to produce its first batch of silver coinage for Canada in 1871. Three years later gold coinage was made for the first time in Birmingham with the famous South African coin, the Burger Pound.

Heaton lever presses were used to re-equip the Royal Mint in 1881 which left Birmingham relying on foreign orders to survive. A contract to build and fit out the Canton Mint in 1887 helped this plight and the venture was a great success.

Ralph III, near to retirement, put the company up as a limited liability company and thus it became The Mint, Birmingham Limited. Ralph IV became Managing Director and other family members took over managerial posts on Ralph III's death in 1891. The mint's output increased for the period from 1889 to 1922 when the empire demanded more coins.

The biggest order for a private mint, at any one time from any one body was placed by Russia from 1896 to 1898 when she needed 110 million copper coins per annum.

Orders also came from Brazil, Mexico and Egypt which kept the mint thriving. In 1912 the Heaton monopoly of Royal Mint orders was broken by the King's Norton Metal Co.Ltd. which has shared production with the Birmingham Mint ever since.

With the outbreak of the First World War minting slowed down and was replaced by the production of brass strips and copper tubing for munition works in the War Effort. 1919 saw the last U.K. issue struck using the Heaton 'H' mintmark and in 1920, Ralph IV retired and W.E. Bromet took charge of the mint. Ralph V joined the firm in 1922 as a commercial, not a managerial employee.

The end of an era came in 1923 when the Royal

Mint first started to mint coins for markets beyond the boundaries of the British Empire on a large scale and could then exercise its power over what type of work Birmingham's private mint would do. This blow marked the start of Bromet's reign which was to end on an equally grey note in the throes of the Great Depression. This period was disastrous for the mint as a profit-making entity, 1929 being the acme of the Depression when coin orders and share dividends dropped to nil or thereabouts.

When Mr. W.F. Brazener took over as Managing Director of the company after 1935 he put the business back on its feet by changing production emphasis from coinage to rolled metals. With the advent of the Second World War, war materials were once again the order of the day. After the war, the mint took a while to recover from being so run-down because it had suffered some blast damage and a great slump in profitable output.

The 1950's saw a low coinage output which recovered with the rest of the company during the 1960's. Brazener retired in 1960 and William Raymond Pearce King took over control. Ralph V retired as Secretary to the company in 1962. Blanks for decimalisation increased output during the period 1968—71 and new machinery was installed to cope with this. A takeover bid by E. and M.P. Smith was thwarted by shareholders in 1963 and the company went from strength to strength with increased skills and good management.

1970 marked the 120th anniversary of the company as the oldest and largest private mint in existence. Mr. King retired in 1973 and was succeeded by Mr. Colin Perry.

During this era of change, coinage again became the largest single activity in the mint and the company was renamed The Birmingham Mint Limited in 1974. Modernisation of the Heaton presses to H.M.E. coin presses and a change in the factory layout to maximise efficiency took place in the late 70's.

Press work in metals became a subsidiary line for the mint in 1980 and other changes were seen in the addition of a new rolling mill and annealing plant, and also the reconstruction of the company. The Birmingham Mint companies which come under this umbrella term function individually in coining, button, badge and medal-making, pressing, die-making and electro-precision work.

The mint still supplies blanks to India and some ex-colonies, and despite these old links, the company is continuing to prove that diversity means strength, with

The Birmingham Mint

Machinery used at various stages of coin manufacturing.

Casting

Milling

Rolling & annealing

Blank cleaning

Striking

Counting
and packing

profits at £2.23 million for the end of the last financial year (March, 1987).

The manufacturing process, from casting to final despatch, and the minting, is carried out at the factory itself. A combination of copper, nickel, tin and zinc is alloyed together and cast into 15mm strips which are surface-milled to remove surface oxides and minor surface defects. The milled strips are rolled to the required thickness and annealed to soften the metal and retain metallic gleam. Coin blanks are then punched from the rolled strip and annealed once again. The blanks are cleaned to make them shine and are washed off, polished and dried. They then go through the rimming and edge-making process if the edges of the coins need demarcation. The blanks take their final shape in the high velocity minting or striking machines, a far cry from the machinery employed in the district in general, many years ago, which great-uncle Ted Hopkins described as needing vile language to get the engines going on the part of the machine operator. Ultimately, the coins are counted, packed, and the quantity weighed to check the accuracy of the amount packaged. The coins are then despatched to the various banks.

The requirement for minting coins arose logically, out of a need to identify the place of issue and to be able to retrace and correct deficient coinage. Originally, the private Heaton mint did not need a mintmark because firstly, it was not set up to relieve some of the transportation problems encountered in nationwide distribution, or to be the source of local coinage — on the contrary, it was there to alleviate the acute demand for Empire coinage which weighed heavily on the Royal Mint; secondly, it did not produce gold or silver coins initially; and thirdly all of Heaton's activities were overwatched by the Royal Mint to ensure that he produced coins in accordance with national standards. These were the reasons why Birmingham, unlike other government-run mints who had to answer to the three stipulations, did not need a mintmark.

In practice, however, Birmingham used more mint-marks than any other mint, purely because it had no government specifications to abide by. As a private enterprise, it could choose its mark as the result of a compromise between the mint and the requirements of the client government. Perhaps the world-renowned 'H' mark, always identified with Birmingham, was used as more of a show-piece than a mintmark. It certainly was the symbol of excellence. Hong Kong was the last country to use the mark in 1972. Today this distinguished mark is only used in limited commemorative editions, greatly increasing their elitist value.

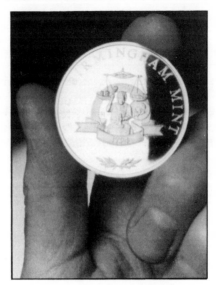

The Mint's house medal.

The British Jewellers' Association:
Its Role and its History

"Behind the cloud the starlight lurks"

These words from a poem by John G. Whittier could not ring more true for the state of the trade than when the light for the future, the Jewellers' Association, was set up in 1887. Amid crime, insolvency, poor trading, disorganisation and lack of skill in 1885 and 1886, a group of attentive businessmen wrote and called for meetings in the trade which resulted in the formation of the first permanent organised body to preside over the trade. The Association elected its first Committee and resolved to make positive steps forward for the trade. It was agreed that its primary objectives should be:

1. To promote art and technical education.
2. To secure uniformity of action in cases of failure.
3. To watch legislation affecting the Trade.
4. To secure prosecution of thieves and receivers.
5. To assist in the development of foreign and colonial trade.
6. To seek through Parliament or other competent authority the removal of all restrictions upon, or the support of all measures for the development of trade.

Membership grew steadily and the Association was finally incorporated with help from Joseph Chamberlain as a Limited Company in 1901. The search for a suitable site began as the establishment grew and after a succession of rented properties, numbers 27 and 27a Frederick Street were taken on.

In 1914, trade machinery manufacturers and silver-mounted leathergoods manufacturers were allowed membership and in 1917 a separate Federation for The Gold, Silver, Electro-plate and Allied Trades Manufacturers was amalgamated with the Association.

With the advent of the First World War the trade capitalised on the weakening of German strongholds in the jewellery market and had a successful collection tour around South America. At the same time, heavy restrictions were imposed upon the industry and manpower

31

The Association Building in 1937

The Federation building in 1987

suffered heavy losses. These were grim times. The trade surfaced from the war and turned over a new leaf with re-organisation of the Association, instigated by the upsurge in trade unionism. The Association was then in a position to deal fairly with unions and employers and to keep relations harmonious.

The Birmingham branch of the jewellers' union formulated guide lines for work in the trade; weekly working hours, minimum wage rates, classification of skilled, semi-skilled and unskilled workers and also trade sections, which have increased from seven to twelve over the years. These sections look after all aspects of jewellery and silversmithing work.

These new regulations brought an end to the 54-hour working week experienced in my great-grandfather's era. Today the Association stipulates a 5-day, 39-hour week in its most recent Wages Agreement. The effects of the original regulations went further, too. My great-uncle's words "labour could do what they liked in those days" in reference to his father who "wasn't easy to get on with!" no longer applied. Workers could no longer up and walk-out after a row. Such upsets are now governed by statutes like The Employment Protection (Consolidation) Act 1978.

On top of this, the lowest rate of pay was also laid down in the new requirements. Pay is still something agreed upon by employer and employee but jobs a e graded and classified more specifically now, and guide-lines are set down to dictate the minimum rate of pay. The situation for trainees, or apprentices as they used to be called, has also altered completely as a result of the post-war re-organisation.

The indentures of my great grandfather show that in 1887 as an apprentice stamper, he earned the equivalent of 45 modern pence per week, which was raised to 75 pence a week by the end of the 5-year apprenticeship. At 18 he was a fully skilled stamper. Today trainees must be between 16 and 16 and a half and their apprenticeship lasts from 3 to 5 years. They are paid a minimum wage which increases with each year of training and rises in line with a skilled adult's wage increase. My great-grand-father's rate of pay remained as laid down in the indent-ures; in the event of a rise then, his wage remained invariable.

After the First World War the Jewellery Quarter saw many changes in make-up, but it was not allowed to reap the benefits from this because of the Great Depression

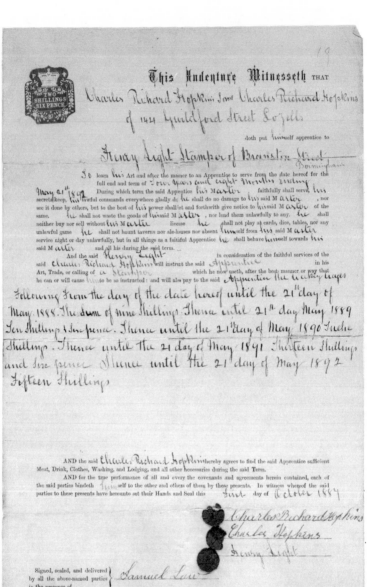

A copy of the author's great-grandfather's indentures of 1887 to
become an apprentice stamper.

which hit Britain through the 20's and early 30's. The Association improved links abroad in 1926 by joining the International Jewellery and Silverware Bureau whereas links with authorities at home were not so choice. The Association had wrangles with the Government over imported wares and tariffs placed upon these goods which were too high. The Association came out victorious.

In 1934 the Metal Finishing Association was established in its own right to cater for its own needs. In the same year, the Junior Council, now called the Young Exectutives' Council, was established with a view to grooming men for sitting on the Association's Executive Committee and raising cash for the Benevolent Fund, set up in 1939 by the Association to aid and provide entertainment for employees in retirement. A trade magazine was also issued for the first time as the culmination of previous smaller ventures. The 'British Jeweller' magazine is still prospering today, as are many other publicity projects both those with histories and the relatively contemporary enterprises. Examples of these are:

The Trade Promotion Services Ltd., set up in 1954, which instigates many of the fairs and exhibitions which take place within the trade, and also

The Buyer's Guide, set up in 1914 which now represents the entire Federation on an international basis and is flourishing today.

The Association celebrated its Golden Jubilee in 1937 with various grandiose events – an exhibition, a Ball, several presentations to royalty and one to the Lord Mayor marked just three of these occasions.

Directly preceding the outbreak of the Second World War, the Association opened a London office for use by members to forward and receive messages and this enabled the Electro-Platers' and Enamellers' section of the trade to join the Association.

The War itself took an immediate stranglehold on the industry with controls on metal consumption and the introduction in 1940 of Purchase Tax, intended to be a temporary measure. This did, in fact, last about thirty years; it came down heavily on deals between registered bodies and the unregistered retail outlets and was not replaced until V.A.T. was introduced in 1973, when the U.K. entered the E.E.C. This was a great burden off the shoulders of the industry and also opened doors to freer trade with E.E.C. countries.

The Board of Trade introduced tight restrictions all through the war years commissioning munition work in manufactories, introducing price restrictions, only lifted in 1949, reducing wedding rings to 9 ct gold, no more, no less and making them, like gold, silver, platinum, diamonds and alarm clocks, virtually non-existent.

Recruitment by the Ministry of Labour included at least half of all workers, crippling the whole trade in the same way as during The Great War. The position of the trade in 1946 was one of all-pervading hopelessness, except for the glimmer of optimism which remained within the Association.

1943 marked the Association's initial efforts to provide for a better future when it became a national organisation including a full-time London branch and a Scottish Area Section. At this time, it also began to consider post-war reconstruction in the shape of a flatted factory which did not materialise until 1971 when the Hockley Centre opened its doors.

The Association became a joint enterprise with the Goldsmiths, Silversmiths, Horological and Kindred Trades in 1946, the Fancy Goods Association was taken in as a new section in 1948, and in the same year re-organisation of membership procedures and committee constitutions took place.

A Grant of Arms was given to the Association in 1950. The first national conference was held in 1955 and these have continued sporadically ever since. In the same year the Silver Collection was begun which now stands as a collection of commissioned items commemorating some important occasions, some as a tribute to the silver industry, like the new piece which celebrates the Association's centenary.

As the Association moved towards contemporary years, it enjoyed, and still enjoys, a healthy relationship with The International Jewellery Association and it took a positive step forward in 1970 when the B.J.A. and all associated bodies came under one blanket term of the British Jewellery and Giftware Federation Ltd.

A Designers' Trade Section was established by the Federation in 1976 to bring designers and manufacturers closer together. In 1979 the Association worked in conjunction with the Council to forward redevelopment plans which have since become the most recent success story in the Jewellery Quarter. The Federation has also instigated Trade Fair Panels with the increasing number of exhibitions over the last decade, with the aim of

Photograph of the family of Charles Hopkins, great grandfather
of the author, taken during the First World War.
All the boys in the family began their working lives in the Jewellery
Quarter.   The two eldest sons (standing) lost their lives during the
war.   Great-Uncle Ted, now aged 87 is seated second on the left.

The interior of the original schoolroom in the Vittoria Street
School as seen in 1891.

creating understanding between organisers and exhibitors and a sounding board for exhibitors so that they can improve the deal for buyers.

Besides representing the Jewellery trade in an official capacity, and offering it intramural cushioning-like Trade Protection, Debt Collection, the Benevolent Fund, and an Export Department which is instrumental in making a success of foreign exhibitions, the Association also moves in social circles. It represents and it entertains, thus maintaining the informal atmosphere prevalent in the trade as a whole. The 1987 banquet, the dances and the various golf competitions and luncheons are all popular events which help to bring people together from different sections of the trade.

Finally the Association played a major role in setting up a formal education for apprentice jewellers. This was in compliance with the Association's original aims, which included the promotion of "art and technical education".

In March, 1888 art classes were begun in the Jewellery Quarter itself, in Ellen Street, a branch of the Birmingham Municipal School of Art and the Association offered 50% of cost of tuition fees for members sending employees for instruction. Sixty pupils enrolled initially and in 1889 the first ever prize-giving ceremony took place for the best students. It is possible although the Jewellers' School and family records could not provide the evidence to back up this theory, that the C.C. Hopkins who won the 1st prize of £1 in this ceremony for "free-hand drawing from diagrams selected by the Head Master, the competition to occupy 3 evenings", is a relative of mine. This is feasible because my great-grandfather Hopkins and the brothers of his approximate age all started in the trade at around this time.

Soon after this, classes grew to such an extent that the Association had to move the School to new premises. A report was sent to the City Council requesting help for this and suggesting a move to 82 and 84 Vittoria Street with the necessary refitting to adapt the building for instruction. The report from the Association's Museum and School of Art Committee also included persuasive statistics which indicated the strength of the jewellery industry at that time, pointing to the necessity of re-housing the school. It concluded: "We have in our City an industry, comprised within a very limited area, which annually works up material of a total value of nearly £2,000,000".

The Committee achieved its goal and preparations for

The centenary silver centrepiece designed by Mike Berry (left)
with right, silversmith Jimmy Butler.

the new Technical School began. The Assay Office donated £500 for equipment and this sum increased annually in line with profits made from the Office. The Committee agreed that classes taught would include many aspects of jewellery production, that the interior form of the school should follow their specifications, that classes should "commence at 6.30 p.m. and close at 8 p.m.", that pupils should attend drawing school one night out of three and that they should wear uniform blouses.

The new Jewellers' Technical School opened its doors on 18th September, 1890, occupying the two-storey building which had been W. and J. Randel's manufactory, a local jeweller, on Vittoria Street. The Lord Mayor opened it on this occasion which was attended by representatives of the various bodies involved in the enterprise. The Association selected the school's first teachers and it also asked members to donate money used to help the school's running costs. Individual Association members contributed cash prizes to intensify competition at the school. The first examinations were taken in 1892 and 20 out of the 23 candidates gained certificates at varying levels of achievement. The new school also moved forward by allowing in female pupils. Naturally, they were taught separately, and by a female instructor!

The Birmingham Jewellers' and Silversmiths' Library was set up in 1897, and the following year sons of employers and "the better class of work people" could be taught in the daytime!

Re-organisation took place in the early 1900's and the School was renamed The Municipal School of Art, Vittoria Street School for Jewellers and Silversmiths. In 1906 a third storey was added to the building to accommodate the growing pupil intake. Ex-servicemen were trained after The Great War and to ensure fair representation in all aspects of the trade, the Committee comprised of members from all trade sections after 1921.

A new Junior School opened in Vittoria Street in 1924 for children aged 12—13 offering a three year course with a job on completion if the pupil was selected by an Association member. The curriculum expanded in all areas to meet requirements in the trade and in 1925 the school staged an exhibition, the first in a long-running tradition which is still maintained.

The School's Golden Jubilee in 1939 was marked by the striking of a medal which was to be the prize for the best all-round student each year, and also by a celebratory

Artist's impression of the Jewellers' School around 1937.

dinner. The Second World War forced the school to channel its resources into making gauges for the War Effort and jewellery classes resumed in February, 1945.

The Associations's strong links with the school continue, helping qualified students to enter the industry and further benefiting education by funding the research of Birmingham University students in various ways, including backing investigation into the discovery of a tarnish-free silver alloy.

Links with the Sir John Cass College, London and the Medway School of Art are also strong in relation to course co-ordination. The Association has, in hand with the Manpower Services Commission, drawn up a basis workshop training course for young people in 1980 and a guaranteed job at the end of it. This was dropped in 1981 but restarted as a Youth Training Scheme in 1983.

The Vittoria Street School is now part of Birmingham Polytechnic with around 120 full time and 340 part time students learning skills of the jewellery trade right in the very heart of the Quarter. The wide variety of courses available from the three-dimensional design department of the Polytechnic includes a B.T.E.C. Higher National Diploma course lasting two years in which specialisation in silversmithing, jewellery, horology and engraving can be obtained. There is also a three year B.A. Industrial Design course, a three year British Horological Institute course and various specialist courses which can be taken once a basic qualification has been gained.

Many part time courses take place for trainee jewellers which are trade orientated and some are for the unemployed and those whose interest in jewellery is purely recreational.

The Y.T.S. scheme which, since 1986, has been a two year course, is controlled by the Association and intended to "provide training with basic skills and experience in all aspects of the jewellery and silverware manufacturing industry including horology". The first years' course work includes training on-the-job (i.e. in a working environment) and off-the-job (i.e. in the school workshops). In the second year specialisation in a skill may take place. This scheme is a growing enterprise with second year trainees numbering 27 and the 1987 first year intake numbering over 30.

The emergence of the Association, "the starlight" lurking behind the cloud 100 years ago, has led to the ongoing, forward-looking organisation which is thriving so well today. It has weathered storms in a volatile industry which is prey to recurrent hiccoughs in the shape of fluctuating markets and fashions, but it always triumphs and bounces back. Its position of strength in 1987, its centenary year, reflects its buoyant nature having surfaced from a bad depression in the early eighties. Its attitude is summed up by the headline in August, 1987's edition of 'Federation News'. It reads:

"Here's looking to 2087!"

and is bursting with the optimistic sentiment predominant in the trade at this point in time.

Looking to the Future

As British Jewellery Year, 1987, draws to a close, the fact that the jewellery trade, particularly in Birmingham is moving from strength to strength is quite clear. The British Jewellers' Association and many other experts in the trade have done some crystal ball gazing and ventured to predict that the future looks rosy for the industry. At this point it would be worthwhile trying to analyse in which direction the trade is moving.

Since the recession at the beginning of the 1980's, some manufacturers have been selling jewellery direct to the public from their shop windows, to cut out dependency on retailers who were unwilling to buy stocks which just did not sell when the economy was at a low ebb. Now that trade has picked up once again these shops are still actively trading and look as though they are here to stay.

The trends visible in the trade generally are showing that 18 ct gold is having a revival and that a departure from purely traditional styles of jewellery is taking place. Modern designs and fashion jewellery are becoming more widespread as many more art and design graduates set up business in the trade and have an influence on the style of jewellery worn, at both ends of the market's price scale.

In 1988 it is intended that a blitz of promotional work should be directed towards the somewhat unexploited French market, with special emphasis on Birmingham's twin town, Lyon. The fact that jewellery production is one of Britain's major sources of wealth, worth an estimated £1.2 billion at retail price, makes jewellery a precious commodity for Britain in more ways than one. According to the healthy Assay Office and Mint figures mentioned in previous chapters, this picture is not going to change. The Chairman of the B.J.A., Mr. John Todd summarises the outlook in this way:

"Improvements in design, quality and finish have made it possible for British Jewellery and silverware

Modern-day design rings.

to compete successfully on all levels with Europe and the rest of the world. These improvements, together with changing trends in fashion and an expanding economy, enhance industry optimism and point towards a bright future for the industry."

Having outlined the short term plans which also include the conclusion of the Association's centenary festivities — a commemorative service at St. Paul's church, 'The Jewellers' church', the annual November students' award ceremony and finally a special Christmas dinner dance — the long term predictions for the trade have also been given by several authorities in the industry.

A variety of views have been expressed, but many theories coincide on certain points. In brief, they say this. As well as some European competition, Eastern markets, for instance Thailand, China and Japan are predicted to become the forerunners in the industry. Hallmarking is forecast to become a worldwide safeguard and there are specific probabilities which will doubtless have a great effect on the industry on an international basis.

Ever-improving communications will make the world shrink and necessitate an acute awareness of the industry moving in international circles. Vast technological advancements will lead to greatly improved efficiency and stiffer competition. Lasers will be used in areas such as soldering and the key to Britain's continuing success story must be for her to exploit her excellent reputation and give her quality designers the widest freedom so that traditions and conservative attitudes in the trade can be broken down. Without the ability to accept change, to put her strong points to maximum use, and to use aggression in marketing, Britain cannot hope to stay in the upper reaches of the international jewellery league. Complacency must become a thing of the past and the will to unite and work together must prevail. The pursuit of excellence in all fields by collective associate bodies and individual craftsmen is also an inherent ingredient for success. This may mean abolishing 9 ct gold or simply improving both ends of the market scale so that customers are offered a quality choice at each end of the price range, and pehaps also a choice inbetween these two extremes, so opening up new territory for the trade.

In brief, expansion, enterprise, enthusiasm, expertise and excellence are the ingredients necessary for the years leading up to 2000 to be successful. This is indeed sound advice and inspired foresight from authorities within the trade itself.   Steps are being taken in the right direction with the City Council's commitment to improving the buildings and environment in the Jewellery Quarter.

The Council hopes it will soon be an impressive tourist attraction as much improvement work has already been completed in the area.

Over 370 projects have been accomplished since 1980 when the district was declared an industrial improvement area.   The improvements have cost around £11 million to date, the bulk of the money coming from the private sector, and funds are still available as plans for the new business Convention Centre and a link up to the Quarter to make it a tourist mecca surge forward.

In February, 1987, one of the most recent major refurbishment projects was completed and the improved building, Anvic House, officially opened.   The three-storey Victorian building now houses 11 workshop units and is another success story of the "get-up-and-go attitude" prevalent in the trade at the moment.

This drive towards recognition of the Quarter's potential, besides creating 600 new jobs and helping to secure thousands more, has also led to a property Mini Boom, directly linked with the trade's economic prosperity at the present time.   The arrival of tourism in The Quarter and the prospect of expansion in this area has brought the trade much more into the public eye.   It must capitalise on this and its other assets in order to realise a future of well-being which will hopefully fulfil and surpass the predictions made for it.   This will be achieved if the industry continues to effuse self-confidence.

The Jewellery Quarter has a unique place to fill in the industrial history of the Midlands and the country as a whole.   It is an example of the inter-dependence of crafts linked to the individuality of craftsmanship that could only arise out of the apparent accidents of the demands of time and place.   Its influence is far-reaching and the very nature of the typical Brummie — individualistic, proud and resourceful has much to do with its industrial past.   This area is now rightly considered an important part of our national heritage.   The demands of time and place in 1987 point to continuing prosperity for the Jewellery Quarter ruling out any possibility of mindless neglect or bureau-cratic bulldozing in the future.

Bibliography

1. A walk in the Jewellery Quarter :
   by the Victorian Society

2. Proposals for conservation in Birmingham's Jewellery Quarter:
   by the Victorian Society

3. Birmingham and its jewellery:
   by John Foster Fraser

4. The evolution of an urban craft:— the gold, silver and allied trades of the West Midlands:
   by Clive Gilbert

5. Learning about heraldry:
   by A.E. Priestley

6. Birmingham gold and silver, 1773—1973:
   compiled by the Birmingham City Museum & Art Gallery

7. The Jewellers' War effort:
   compiled by the Birmingham Jewellers' and Silver-smiths' Association

8. Victorian Birmingham:
   by Victor Skipp

9. Supplement to the Dial:
   by J.C. Roche

10. The British Jewellers' Association — 100 years of Service:
    by Shelley Nott

11. The Silversmiths of Birmingham:
    by K. Crisp Jones

12. Matthew Boulton and the toymakers:
    Catalogue of Exhibition at Goldsmiths Hall, London — November 1982

13. A numesmatic history of the Birmingham Mint:
    By T.O. Sweeney

14. The Goldsmith's Review Vol 1—3:
    Compilation of articles.

15. Jewellery Quarter Edition for Brum Trail No.6:
    compiled by Clive Gilbert

TERMS USED IN THE JEWELLERY TRADE

Annealing — the softening of hardened metal through a heating process.

Blocking — the shaping of silver by hammering with a ball-ended sinking hammer or a pear-shaped blocking mallet.

Burnishing — the polishing of delicate or awkward sections of metal using agates, stones or highly polished metal tools.

Casting — the moulding of liquid metal into the shape which it takes from the cast.

Chasing — two-dimensional chasing is a process similar to engraving but which marks the metal's surface without cutting away, but by pushing.
Repousse chasing represents the same tracing process, only carried out on a three-dimensional object.

Die Sinking — the chiselling of dies used to make tools, medals, coins etc.

Electroplating — the depositing of pure silver on to baser metal in an electrical process which produces silver plate.

Engraving — the cutting away of metal using a graver or some other specific tool for a decorative or functional purpose.   Many mass-produced articles are engraved mechanically.

Enamelling — the adding of colour to chased, stamped or engraved metal articles by a process of fusion.   Individual processes are the Champleve, the Basse-taille, the Cloisonne, the Plique a Jour and the Limoges methods, the latter being the simple painting of a prepared surface with enamel.

Electrogilding — the same process as silver electroplating, but using gold, not silver anodes and cyanide solution. This gives gold plate.

Modelling — the use of materials used for casting patterns or models.

Piercing — the shaping of an article for decoration or otherwise in which a piercing saw is used.   Dies or a fly press are used for this process in mass production.

Planishing — the hammering of an article after the raising process in order to give the metal a smoother finish.

Polishing — the process of giving lustre to the finished metal.   Silver is sanded with fine sand or pumice powder

49

and an organic lubricant and then polished on a felted bob or wheel which revolves rapidly. Final polishing is done manually.

Raising — the raising of the surface of an article with a hammer. This process takes place if the article is too deep to be blocked.

Soldering — clean parts are joined together in this process by heat and solder.

Spinning — the process of raising run mechanically.

Stamping — the shaping of metal by placing it over a female die and bringing the male die down upon the metal heavily with a drop stamp, fly or hydraulic press and so shaping the metal.

PROFILE OF THE AUTHOR

Alison Gledhill — born — Birmingham 1st January 1969. She attended St. Martin's School, Solihull until 1985 then Solihull School Sixth form which she left in July 1987.

She will begin reading for a degree in Modern and Mediaeval languages at St. John's College, Cambridge in October 1988.

Alison is a keen sports woman and especially enjoys swimming at a competitive level.

FORWARD

THE BIRMINGHAM COAT OF ARMS

When the Borough of Birmingham was incorporated in 1838 it adopted the armorial bearings of the de Bermingham family (Lords of the Manor from the Norman Conquest to 1532) as its Seal.

In 1889, when Birmingham was granted city status, it gained the right to add supporters (figures) to the shield. Minor adjustments were made in 1936.

Following boundary reorganisation in 1974 the Royal Borough of Sutton Coldfield became part of the city. A new Coat of Arms was adopted in 1976. The design included a bishop's mitre (commemorating the 16th century Bishop Vesey) and the Tudor rose (marking Henry VIII's granting of a charter in 1528).

Two distinct quarters appear on the shield. The bend of lozenges appears on the shield of an effigy of a de Bermingham Lord in St-Martins-in-the-Bull Ring.

The Coat of Arms was granted by the College of Arms.

BOOKS ON BIRMINGHAM

We hope you have enjoyed reading about Birmingham's Jewellery Quarter.
The following books on Birmingham have already been published by Brewin Books and are available from booksellers throughout the Midlands.

BIRMINGHAM CINEMAS (Foreword by Alton Douglas) Victor Price.
A nostalgic look at the city's cinemas from 1900—1960. The first film show was presented in Aston Manor by showman Pat Collins in the year 1888 and the new printing of this popular book commemorates a hundred years of motion pictures in the City. A4 large size paperback, profusely illustrated £10.95. (Royalties to St. Mary's Hospice, Selly Oak)

OLTON HERITAGE Jean Powrie, Margaret Jordan and Carol Andrews.
The history of a suburb now part of Solihull. The three sections of the book deal with Olton's history, its famous people and places, and life in Victorian and Edwardian times, when Edith Holden wrote and illustrated her famous Diary.
Available in A5 Paperback at £6 or in Hardback at £12.

OLD LADYWOOD REMEMBERED (Foreword by Canon Norman Power) Victor Price.
Our 1987 best seller and now reprinted, Victor Price's book depicts Old Ladywood in a host of photographs and describes life in this friendly busy suburb before redevelopment demolished the little shops and houses for ever.
A5 Paperback, fully illustrated (Royalties to Ladywood Church) £4.95

STEAM ON THE BIRMINGHAM GLOUCESTER LOOP Philip Jarvis.
Philip Jarvis's book describes in pictures the old Midland Railway Line (later L.M.S.) from Birmingham through Barnt Green, Redditch, Studley and Alcester down into Gloucestershire. Every station is illustrated with period photographs and there is a good selection of photographs of steam locomotives, rolling stock and lineside features.
A5 Illustrated. £6.40 (Royalites to St. Stephen's Church, Redditch).

THE ANGEL OF CAMP HILL Joan Stoker
A Tribute to Deirdre McDowell, Headmistress of Holy Trinity Church of England School, Camp Hill, our book describes the life of this great character who extended her role as headmistress far beyond the usual bounds to serve the community.
A5 Paperback £5.95

We have more new titles due for release in 1988 and will forward a full catalogue upon application to:

K.A.F. BREWIN BOOKS, Doric House, Church Street, Studley, Warwickshire.